Original title:
Whispers in the Wisteria

Copyright © 2025 Creative Arts Management OÜ
All rights reserved.

Author: Dexter Sullivan
ISBN HARDBACK: 978-1-80567-391-0
ISBN PAPERBACK: 978-1-80567-690-4

The Lure of Entwined Branches

In the garden of tangled dreams,
Monkeys swing with silly schemes,
Chasing butterflies with tiny nets,
While plotting snacks like popcorn pets.

Bamboo hats on heads so proud,
They gather round, a funny crowd,
Telling tales of grape escape,
While munching leaves in a leafy drape.

Stories in the Shaded Nook

Underneath the leafy arch,
Squirrels hold their fat parade,
Juggling acorns with a spark,
As shadows dance, the sun delayed.

A rabbit hops by, all in a rush,
Joined by a turtle in a hush,
They race to see who can out-chill,
While a sly fox takes a break, just still.

The Tranquility of Curling Vines

Vines twirl round like silly dancers,
Tickling bees with perfumed lances,
They giggle as the flowers bloom,
A vivid space, dispelling gloom.

A snail zooms past, not on a quest,
But for a snack, he knows it best,
He bumps a toad who gives a laugh,
While on the side, ants share a snack.

Whispers of the Hidden Flora

Petals chat beneath the moon,
Rabbits join in with a cartoon,
Mice peek out, they can't resist,
To join the dance, they twist and twist.

A lazy cat joins the fun of night,
Chasing shadows, oh what a sight!
Frogs croak jokes, the laughter swells,
In the garden, all is well.

Dreams in a Floral Haven

In a garden where flowers giggle,
Petals dance with a jolly wiggle.
Bees are buzzing like tiny clowns,
Sipping nectar in sunny gowns.

The daisies play truth or dare,
While vines chase shadows everywhere.
Starlit socks on sleepy bees,
Joking with the rustling leaves.

Secrets of the Twisting Tendrils

Vines twist like a barber's pole,
Telling tales that make you roll.
A cucumber's hat and radish shoes,
The garden holds the silliest views.

Tendrils tickle the snoozing mushrooms,
While daisies hum their silly tunes.
Rabbits laugh at their own long ears,
Giggling as they shift their gears.

Songs of the Swaying Blooms

The flowers sing in perfect tune,
Underneath the watching moon.
Sunflowers wear shades, looking cool,
While tulips chase the butterfly school.

In the breeze, the flowers sway,
Playing hopscotch, come what may.
Carnations giggle with all their might,
As they waltz with the firefly light.

The Language of Lavender Leaves

In lavender fields, jokes take flight,
With leaves that whisper day and night.
Their humor drifts upon the breeze,
Tickling toes of bumbling bees.

Jokes are told by the tulip crew,
Who wear a crown of morning dew.
Laughter echoes 'round the bend,
In a floral world that has no end.

Secrets Cradled by the Vines

Beneath the dancing leaves, I hear,
A squirrel's gossip, loud and clear.
He tells of acorns lost in a game,
A search for snacks, oh, what a shame!

The vines entwine, they giggle tight,
As bees compete in a buzzing fight.
They're tangled up, and so are we,
In nature's jest, we're all carefree.

Embrace of the Scented Night

In twilight's arms, the crickets chat,
Who knew they'd sport a tiny hat?
They serenade the moonlit lawn,
While shadows dance, their laughter drawn.

The stars above roll their bright eyes,
As owls exchange their wise-crack lies.
The flowers bloom, they bloom so bold,
Sharing secrets only night can hold.

Fables of the Flowing Blooms

A blooming flower once told a tale,
Of bumblebees who loved to fail.
With every buzz, they lost their way,
Yet still, they danced and seemed to play.

The daisies laughed, the roses sighed,
As petals twirled, and pollen cried.
Each bloom a comedy of errors,
A garden filled with cheerful terrors.

Serene Shadows of the Soft Violet

In shades of purple, shadows prance,
As moths engage in a wild dance.
They stumble 'round with clumsy grace,
A waltz with nature, a funny chase.

The gentle breeze joins in the fun,
A chorus sung by everyone.
Jokes are cracked in the silver light,
While night unfolds its merry sight.

Silk Like Secrets Entwined

A squirrel in a tutu spins with grace,
While bees wear shades, they dance in place.
The flowers giggle as the breeze draws near,
They chat and chuckle, just like old peers.

The butterflies gossip, flitting around,
Sipping sweet nectar, with no care found.
One says, 'Why do daisies think they're cool?',
Another replies, 'They must've skipped school!'

The Sway of the Enchanted Boughs

The trees are swaying to a silly beat,
Branches waving like they're at a retreat.
A raccoon in pajamas pop-corns nearby,
As birds in tuxedos croon songs from the sky.

Laughter flows gently in this leafy space,
When a squirrel, quite cheeky, takes up the bass.
The fruits roll their eyes, in a fruity refrain,
'It's not easy being the apple of the lane!'

Tranquil Promises in Bloom

A tulip tells tales of a far-off land,
Where bunnies wear glasses and make a band.
The daisies all giggle, the roses look sly,
While daisies hoot, and the orchids just sigh.

Petals, like jesters, dance on the ground,
As pansies plot pranks; oh, what mischief found!
A hive of bees buzzing a raucous tune,
While the sun winks down like a playful cartoon.

Hidden Melodies of the Arbor

In the shade of the leaves, a fiddle plays tunes,
The crickets chirp sweetly, under the moons.
A rabbit wearing a hat jigs on the grass,
While the fireflies flicker, just having a blast.

A joke-telling owl pops out from his nook,
He squints at the flowers, 'Read any good book?'
With chirps and with giggles, the evening unwinds,
Where laughter and light dance, and silliness binds.

Fragments of a Garden Dream

In a spot where daisies play,
A frog rehearses for ballet.
With tiny toes and flailing arms,
He steals the show with his green charms.

A bumblebee dons a tiny hat,
Buzzing 'round like a chubby cat.
He claims the daisies for his own,
While flowers giggle in their throne.

The daisies whisper, 'What a sight!'
As Ladybug sips tea at night.
With spotty dress and dainty grace,
She asks the sun for a bright space.

So in this patch, so full of cheer,
The garden's laughter is all we hear.
With every bloom and buzz so grand,
The world turns light with nature's band.

Dances in the Dappled Light

A squirrel prances, tail on high,
He dodges shadows, oh so spry.
With leaps and twirls on branches wide,
He looks like he's got nothing to hide.

The sunlight giggles through the trees,
As ants march on, proud as you please.
They carry crumbs like treasure grand,
While grasshoppers scale the golden sand.

A dance-off starts with a buzzing crew,
Bees and butterflies join in too.
They flit and flutter, oh so bold,
In this sun-drenched garden, joy unfolds.

So let us sway in this merry light,
Where laughter rings both day and night.
In every corner, a jovial blast,
In dappled dreams, our fun holds fast.

The Enchantment of Olive Green

Amidst the trees where olives gleam,
A raccoon dreams an absurd dream.
With tiny paws and mischief's spark,
He camped beneath an old, wide park.

The owls giggle in their hoots,
As lizards strut in playful suits.
A party starts at half-past four,
When critters gather, they roar for more.

A startled mouse spills lemonade,
While crickets serenade the parade.
Dancing on hills of fragrant grass,
They trip and tumble; oh, what a class!

In olive dreams where laughter thrives,
The flora sways as each one jives.
With every rustle, a curious cheer,
In every nook, good times appear.

Tales from the Cloistered Boughs

Beneath the branches, secrets play,
Where whispers tickle leaves all day.
A squirrel tells a tale of cheese,
While robins giggle in the breeze.

The chipmunks gather for a show,
With acorns as their props in tow.
They juggle seeds and dance around,
Their tiny laughter fills the ground.

A crow on high starts to croon,
Singing tunes atop a moon.
His voice is deep, a feathery beat,
The forest listens, tapping feet.

So here beneath the trees so grand,
The creatures form a merry band.
In cloistered boughs, the stories spread,
With joy and laughter, all are fed.

The Call of the Lush Canopy

The trees wear hats of purple flair,
Beneath them, squirrels have a dare.
They stash their nuts with little glee,
While birds discuss their favorite tea.

Dancing leaves in the lazy breeze,
Invite a march of tiny fleas.
They jig and twirl in bold parade,
While pondering their grand charade.

A raccoon lands on a branch with style,
And all the flowers laugh a while.
They whisper tales of silly pranks,
As nature's misfits toast their flanks.

With every rustle, giggles rise,
From flower beds to sunny skies.
In the lush canopy, they sing,
A joyful ode to spring's wild fling.

Blossoms With a Secret

Petals gossip beneath the sun,
Of secret loves and garden fun.
A bee gets tangled in a tale,
While ladybugs just roll and sail.

With cheeks so bright, the blooms conspire,
To craft a game, a grand desire.
Behind their hues, they play it cool,
Yet every bud can bend the rule.

A beetle steps on tiny toes,
Crafting moves that nobody knows.
Each twist and turn a comical plight,
As blossoms beam with pure delight.

The wind chuckles as it sways,
Enjoying all their frolic plays.
For in this garden, joy's the key,
Of petal pranks and silly glee.

Hidden Voices of the Vine

Beneath the leaves, a secret crew,
Of curling vines in shades of blue.
They share a laugh, a sly remark,
As beetles dance with well-timed spark.

The grapes hold court in tiny hushed tones,
Debating who will steal the bones.
A sly fox drops in with flair,
Declaring he's the best debonair.

Amidst the laughter, a bumblebee,
Winks at flowers, as cute as can be.
He spins a tale of nectar bliss,
While blooms shake their heads and hiss.

A gentle breeze flows through the scene,
Tickling vines—what a fun routine!
In this riot of colors entwined,
The hidden voices are joyfully aligned.

Subtle Notes Among the Blooms

In the soft shade where laughter grows,
The blossoms hum in curious prose.
A snail hosts an evening show,
While flowers clap, putting on a glow.

The daisies gossip, quite a feat,
About a beetle's dance, sort of sweet.
They shake their stems, a rippling sound,
As petals giggle all around.

A mischievous lizard struts with pride,
Claiming he's the jungle's guide.
But lilies roll their eyes to tease,
As grasshoppers form a lively breeze.

While shadows play, the sunlight beams,
Creating an orchestra of dreams.
Among the blooms, in cheeky light,
The subtle notes weave pure delight.

The Echo of Nature's Caress

In the garden, bugs dance around,
A bee with a hat, not making a sound.
Flowers giggle, their petals shake,
They plot a prank on the garden rake.

Under the tree, a squirrel tells jokes,
While mushrooms chuckle, like old folks.
The sun joins in, with a bright little beam,
Causing shadows to linger, like a meme.

A breeze carries laughter, soft and bright,
Leaves rustle gently, in sheer delight.
Nature's stage, where antics play,
Each day's a circus, in a leafy ballet.

So join in the fun, let worries drift,
With giggles in petals, consider it a gift.
In this land of antics, let spirits rise,
Laughter's the key, beneath sunny skies.

Yarn of Petals and Dreams

In a field of daisies, antics unfold,
A snail tells tales, both daring and bold.
With petals like blankets, they gather 'round,
Bumbling bunnies bounce, without making a sound.

A butterfly stitches a gown from the sun,
Rabbits wear spectacles, thinking they're fun.
On a throne made of leaves, a ladybug sits,
Declaring her rule with a flick of her wit.

The breeze brings a melody, playful and sweet,
While ants tap their feet, in their own little beat.
They march in a line, with tiny top hats,
Caterpillars giggle, while dodging those spats.

So dance with the blooms, let laughter take flight,
In a world full of color, everything's bright.
With dreams stitched in petals, embrace the delight,
For nature's a jester, under the starlight.

Tapestry of the Flowering Veil

A hedgehog dons shades, as cool as can be,
As daisies parade, singing with glee.
A fox in a vest, with a wink and a grin,
Dances in circles, inviting us in.

Petals weave tales, as the sun starts to yawn,
Squirrels drive by in a car made of lawn.
They honk with delight, wearing caps on their heads,
While daisies roll laughter, tucked snug in their beds.

Caterpillars debate on what to wear next,
Their fashion is silly, it's truly perplexed.
A butterfly judges, with flair and with pride,
As the blooms giggle softly, watching the ride.

So join in the fun, let your heart feel the thrill,
As nature replays each scene with a skill.
In the tapestry woven with laughter and play,
Life's a great jest, in a wild, charming way.

Tales of the Twilit Flora

In a garden where shadows play,
The flowers gossip in a silly way.
Roses wear hats, and daisies dance,
Sunflowers wink at the evening romance.

A dandelion sneezes, sends seeds in flight,
While violets giggle at the moon's soft light.
Bees buzz by, wearing tiny bow ties,
Tickling leaves, as laughter fills the skies.

Lily pads leap, frogs join the show,
With wobbly hops, putting on a glow.
In this land of blooms, all troubles cease,
Every petal chuckles, sharing joy and peace.

So if you walk where the twilight glows,
Remember, flowers have tales to propose.
They'll whisper antics of a secret quest,
In the realm of petals, they jest and jest.

The Spirit of Dancing Petals

There's a breeze that likes to tango,
With petals pirouetting in a row.
Butterflies twirl in a flirty spree,
As blooms compete for the best marquee.

Marigolds gossip, sharing wild tales,
About bees stealing nectar, and leafy trails.
A peony trips, lands with a thud,
While the others all burst out laughing in mud.

Pansies wear shades, looking so cool,
While wind chimes giggle, breaking the rule.
A sunflower honks as it strikes a pose,
Nature's comedy, with a splash of prose.

So if your heart feels a tad bit blue,
Join the petals in their dance, it's true.
With each little twirl, let laughter ignite,
In the spirit of blooms, everything feels right.

Garden of Starlit Secrets

Underneath the twinkling skies,
The flowers share their nightly lies.
A tulip claims it's a rock star's kin,
While a daisy just grins, joining in.

Lilacs plot with the twinkling stars,
Creating secret clubs with cookies in jars.
The nightingale croons, a serenade sweet,
But the lilies just laugh, tapping their feet.

Frogs hold meetings on lily pads round,
Arguing loudly, who's the best croak sound.
The moon peeks in, with a knowing glance,
As petals burst forth in a whimsical dance.

Each flower's a dreamer, a skit to perform,
Bathing in starlight, creating their norm.
In the garden cloaked with secrets so deep,
Let's join the fun, as laughter takes leap.

Harmonies of the Winding Stems

In a tangle of stems, a band takes flight,
Each flower's a player, performing at night.
Vines strum melodies, soft and sweet,
While petals tap out a rhythmic beat.

Cacti join in, with a prickly beatbox,
Dancing around in their quirky frocks.
Orchids sway gently, in a grand ballet,
While cosmos giggle, stealing the play.

Through laughter and music, the garden hums,
As the night wraps around, their joy now drums.
With every bloom cooling off summer's heat,
Join in the fun, let your heart skip a beat.

So close your eyes, let the magic begin,
In harmonies sweet, you'll feel the grin.
For in this realm of playful delight,
Every leaf's a note, dancing in the night.

Songs of Serenity in Bloom

In the garden where shadows play,
Sneaky squirrels plot their fray.
A frog leaps high, but lands all wrong,
An audience laughs, they won't be long.

Bees hum tunes that sound like jazz,
While flowers sway, showing some pizzazz.
A raccoon dances, moonlit in style,
Chasing his tail, nonchalant with a smile.

Petals fall, a confetti parade,
Each step brings joy, and none are afraid.
Laughter lingers, on petals it rides,
In this lively bloom, humor abides.

Sunset giggles light up the sky,
As crickets chirp their lullaby.
In the heart of the green, all is bright,
Even nature finds joy in the night.

Reveries Within the Garden's Embrace

In a garden where giggles peek,
A gnome sings softly, his voice unique.
Next to him sits a toad so bold,
Who croaks the truth, or so I'm told.

Butterflies flutter, in outfits so grand,
They strut like models upon the land.
Frogs have a ball, on lily pads splash,
Each dance step, a funny little crash.

Sunflowers bow to ticklish bees,
Who buzz with laughter, riding the breeze.
They chat about honey and dance on a whim,
While daisies giggle at the sight of him.

The rainbow paints whispers across the sky,
As flowers chime in with a joyful sigh.
In this embrace of giggles and glee,
Even the worms join in for a spree.

The Heartbeat of the Blossoms

A bud bursts open with a yawn so wide,
A weary bee takes a moment to hide.
Pollen tickles, and soon it will sneeze,
Sending forth laughter on the soft breeze.

A ladybug winks, her spots all in line,
While ants march in step, oh how they dine!
Each leaf a stage for nature's delight,
Performing antics till fall of night.

Petunias gossip, spreading the tale,
Of a squirrel who tried to overtake a snail.
Neither quick, nor sly—just a friendly race,
Which left both breathless, in a laughing place.

The roots tap dance 'neath the soil's great hold,
While breezes weave stories, both silly and bold.
In the heart of this bloom, joy takes its stand,
With laughter echoing across the land.

Messages Carried on the Breeze

A dandelion puff takes flight with a cheer,
Spreading secret giggles far and near.
Each seed a joke whispered in haste,
As the wind carries laughter—oh what a taste!

Sunlight chuckles, as it tickles the grass,
While shadows play hide and seek with sass.
A peacock struts, feathers all aglow,
As if he's the star of a wacky show.

The rhododendrons gossip, bloom after bloom,
Making funny faces in nature's room.
They tease the roses for being so prim,
While daisies giggle, they dance on a whim.

Hummingbirds zip in a zigzag of speed,
Creating a comedy—oh what a lead!
In this fragrant theater, laughter finds wings,
As petals sway gently, joyfully flings.

Secrets Beneath the Blossoms

Behind the blooms, secrets giggle,
A squirrel steals nuts, avoids a wiggle.
Petals dance, a secret show,
Where laughter hides and breezes blow.

Beneath the leaves, a cat does prance,
Chasing shadows, lost in chance.
A bee hums tunes, the flowers sway,
In this quirky garden, all play.

The gnomes grumble, their hats askew,
"Did you hear what the snail just knew?"
Rainbows peek through playful vines,
In this chaos, joy defines.

Laughter blurs the lines of day,
As garden critters lead the way.
With petals soft and mischief grand,
Life's secrets flourish hand in hand.

Echoes of Sweet Serenity

In a patch of peace, frogs croak tunes,
While daisies gossip under the moons.
A raccoon slips, trying to spy,
While butterflies laugh and flutter by.

Chirping crickets, with such flair,
Debate the best flights through the air.
Leaves rustle with stories untold,
As squirrels chuckle, a sight to behold.

A ladybug flaunts her red spots,
While a hedgehog ties up his knots.
Echoes of hilarity float about,
In the stillness, the garden shouts.

With whimsical blooms and playful skies,
Nature's humor always complies.
In sweet serenity, giggles entwine,
A secret joke for hearts that dine.

Veils of Lavender Light

In shadows cast by lavender bloom,
A chubby bunny searches for room.
Hopping lightly, he spies the prize,
A carrot hidden under the skies.

The sunlight dances on petals fair,
While dragonflies twirl without care.
A tiny worm wears a sunhat too,
Thinking he's the coolest of the crew.

With giggles carried on breezy sighs,
The garden crew schemes with bright eyes.
A hedgehog shimmies, a ridiculous sight,
Underneath the soft, veiled light.

Petals whisper jokes to the ground,
In the silliness, peace is found.
With laughter stitched into each vein,
Life blooms bright, devoid of pain.

Murmurs in the Botanical Canopy

In the canopy, secrets rise,
As chubby squirrels share their pies.
A parrot squawks, "Who's stealing snacks?"
The chatter swells from leafy tracks.

Treetops hide a monkey's show,
With flips and twists, he steals the glow.
Lions lounge, dreaming of fun,
While butterflies cheer as they run.

Giggling vines climb high, oh dear,
Tickling each branch with laughter clear.
Murmurs dance through branches wide,
Where silly antics cannot hide.

Under green shade, joy's parade,
Nature's quirks in sunlight played.
In this canopy, mirth takes flight,
A world aglow in pure delight.

Shadows in Blooming Beauty

In the garden of secrets, plants do conspire,
Giggling flowers, stretching ever higher.
They plan a party with bees for a dance,
While curious bunnies peek for a chance.

The daisies dressed up in their yellow best,
Sporting little hats, they truly jest.
Tulips are gossiping, oh what a scene,
About that sly fox who pranced through green.

Even the roses roll their eyes with glee,
As a snail races past, oh what a spree!
They chuckle at raindrops painting the ground,
Nature's own pranksters, beauty unbound.

So if you stroll past this flowery show,
Listen closely, you might hear them glow.
For amidst the blooms, a light-hearted jest,
In shadows of beauty, they surely rest.

Serenade of the Twining Vines

The vines twist and turn with a flair so grand,
Offering shade with a touch of a hand.
They sing to the breeze with a rustling tune,
Confusing the daisies that dance with the moon.

Grapes giggle wildly, swaying in time,
As caterpillars shuffle in antics sublime.
One claims he can wallop a worm in a race,
While the squirrels all watch with a grin on their face.

A lizard in shades of dazzling green,
Pretends he's the star of this leafy scene.
They cheer as he struts on his tiny stout legs,
Claiming he's got the best groove of the dregs.

The sun peeks in, giving all a warm hug,
While crickets compose with a joyful shrug.
In the tangle of life, they find joy inside,
A serenade shared where spirits abide.

The Silence of Petaled Dreams

Under the moon, the blooms seem to giggle,
As night's cool embrace makes the petals wiggle.
Tulips declare, 'We'll catch a few Z's!'
While daisies burst forth with a round of 'Cheese!'

A dreaming bee buzzes with snacks on his mind,
Yet tumbles and fumbles, oh my, how unkind!
He claims he's the king, yet his crown's made of dew,
While petals all chuckle, 'Who knew he was blue?'

Moths flutter by, dressed in grand evening wear,
As butterflies tease, 'Do you come from the fair?'
In shadows of petals, a riotous glee,
As the garden comes alive with mirthful decree.

So don't let the night fool you, dear friend of the light,
For blooms hold their party long into the night.
In the silence of dreams that drift through the air,
Every flower joins in with laughter to share.

Dance of the Hanging Flowers

From branches above, the blooms sway and swing,
Each petal a dancer, with joy they all sing.
They chatter in laughter, spun tales of delight,
While teasing the pollen that drifts through the night.

"Oh look at that spider!" a bloom starts to shout,
"He thinks he's so clever, we'll just twist about!"
The petals laugh loudly, their colors ablaze,
As the spider, confused, winds up in a daze.

The colors all twirl, it's a floral ballet,
With every bright hue, they glide and they sway.
Petunias proclaim, "We've never felt freer!
Let's steal this show, we're the real crowd-pleaser!"

So if you should wander where flowers find fun,
You'll witness a spectacle under the sun.
In this dance of life, all pranks are laid bare,
Blooming with laughter in the soft summer air.

Echoing Stories Among the Leaves

In the garden where gossip grows,
Plants gossip louder than your nose.
The lilies chuckle, the daisies chat,
While squirrels debate who's fatter than fat.

The breeze steals secrets from boughs above,
A tale about a lovesick dove.
With each rustling leaf, stories unfold,
Of cats that dance and flowers bold.

Hilarity blooms in the midday glow,
As daisies tell jokes the peonies know.
A tulip slips, falls flat on its face,
And everyone giggles at the awkward grace.

So listen close, to the laughter around,
In this lively place, joy can be found.
Every petal has tales ripe for a feast,
Where the most serious flower is just the least.

Secrets of Silken Shadows

Underneath the boughs clad in green,
A spider spins stories unseen.
Adventures of ants who never agree,
And a butterfly's quest for a cup of tea.

Each shadowy nook holds a giggling tale,
Of beetles in bow ties, oh what a scale!
Then there's the worm, who's a fashion trend,
Swearing that dirt makes the best blend.

The mushrooms convene, hats tipped with flair,
Secrets exchanged in the cool evening air.
With twinkling eyes, they spout jokes so spry,
About frogs who dream of reaching the sky.

A whispering breeze, playful and spry,
As laughter cascades where the shadows lie.
Gather around for this spectacle bright,
Where the garden unfolds its delight.

The Glistening Cloak of Dusk

As twilight dances, colors collide,
Crickets are chirping and bugs take pride.
In the softening light, fireflies compete,
To be the star on the evening's heartbeat.

The roses roll in laughter and cheer,
About the way that the moon's a mere sphere.
While shadows of slugs, with a swagger so bold,
Claim they once fought a dragon of gold.

The stars start to giggle, all blink and twinkle,
As night drapes its cloak and begins to sprinkle.
The garden grows wild with tales to regale,
Of pretentious plants and their absurd fail.

So join in this frolic, as twilight descends,
Where night creatures chatter and laughter transcends.
In the glistening dark, let your spirit be free,
In this humorous plot, where all bloom with glee.

Memories Sown in Petal Dust

Among the petals where laughter does swell,
Time spins tales only flowers can tell.
With each playful swirl of the springtime breeze,
Petals share secrets with mischievous tease.

A daffodil winks, "I'm the first of my kind!"
While the pansies plot to prank the blind.
The lilacs chuckle, "We're royalty, see?
But don't tell the roses; they think they're the key!"

In soft shades of pink, stories collide,
Of bees with bad jokes who won't be denied.
Each colorful bloom has a grin on its face,
Making humor bloom in this joyful place.

So come join the dance of whims in the air,
Where petals hold truths that no one can bear.
In memories sown, let the laughter take flight,
As flowers throw parties beneath the starlight.

Lullabies of the Leafy Cloak

A squirrel in a top hat, quite a sight,
Dances in shadows, avoiding the light.
He sings to the breeze, his tune is quite spry,
With acorns as maracas, he's ready to fly.

The flowers chuckle, their petals take flight,
While bees don their shades, looking oh-so-right.
They buzz in a chorus, a comical hum,
As nature's oddball band plays a wacky drum.

A robin with glasses reads poetry there,
Each word makes a blossom burst into flare.
The branches are giggling, the grass starts to sway,
As laughter spills out in a whimsical way.

So frolic with friends in this leafy retreat,
Where the grass is a dance floor, the air is a treat.
Join in the fun, let your worries all flee,
In this garden of chuckles, forever be free.

Murmurs of the Enfolding Foliage

The rabbits engage in a raucous debate,
While hedgehogs are rolling, it's a curious fate.
They're all dressed in costumes, it's quite the affair,
With daisies for hats and a dandelion flare.

The bushes are gossiping, sharing their views,
While butterflies giggle, flaunting their hues.
A worm with a bow tie recites little jokes,
The laughter erupts, bring in the oak folks.

A tortoise sipping tea, slow and quite nice,
Takes bets on the races, oh, wouldn't that suffice?
The wind's got a snicker, leaves rustle and dance,
While daisies are tossing their heads in a trance.

Join this grand party of giggles and glee,
In the curl of the branches, where all are carefree.
May laughter surround you and joy fill your day,
In this leafy abode, come and frolic away.

The Sound of Blooming Secrets

In the thicket, a cricket is planning a play,
With a cast of odd flowers that come out to sway.
A violet leads scenes, while a daisy's a star,
They strut and they prance, forget who you are.

A snail with a trumpet, not ready to quit,
Plays tunes that can tickle, a sound that's a hit.
While the daisies retreat, it's a comical rift,
Every bloom in the garden just can't help but lift.

A patch of old daisies share jokes of their youth,
While lilacs add spice, none could tell a truth.
With chuckles and sidesteps, each leaf has a role,
As laughter unravels from nature's own soul.

So come for the show, and bring all your cheer,
In the heart of the blooms, there's nothing to fear.
The silly old whispers will lead you astray,
In the garden of giggles, come dance on your way.

Serenades from the Hidden Grove

In the grove where the giggles are stylishly loud,
A bear in a tutu is dancing, so proud.
He twirls 'round the trees, with a grin on his face,
Each move sends the bunnies into a mad race.

The crows on their branches act as the judges,
Counting each twirl, shouting out all their grudges.
A hedgehog flips pancakes, a breakfast parade,
While the leaves join in laughter, no one's afraid.

A moose with a cape roots for everyone here,
Cheering with gusto, spreading joy and good cheer.
With raccoons decorating the stage with delight,
In this hidden arena, all's perfectly right.

So gather your friends where the antics unfold,
In this muscular grove, where the stories are told.
Leave worries behind you, embrace all the fun,
In this merry old refuge, where all are as one.

Tales Told by the Flowering Vines

In the garden, where blooms do jive,
The vines gossip, feeling alive.
They snicker and giggle, take a chance,
Sharing secrets with every dance.

A bee buzzes past with a comical frown,
Wearing a crown, feeling like a clown.
As petals sway, they start to tease,
"Who wore that shade? It's sure to freeze!"

An old tree chuckles, roots deep in debate,
"Those daisies think they're the ones to inflate!"
The vines roll their eyes, quite unimpressed,
"Well, let's just say they put us to rest!"

But as the sun sets, the laughter glows,
A chorus of giggles in soft, playful flows.
When night falls gently, they all take a bow,
With vines telling tales, it's quite the row!

Secret Serenades of the Arbor

Under the arbor, so cozy and sweet,
The leaves share stories, a musical treat.
With rustling tones, they begin to hum,
About the car, the tree, and a runaway drum!

A squirrel joins in, with a nutty design,
Tapping his paws, he's keeping good time.
Branches sway softly, rhythm in line,
While flowers giggle at their own vine.

The moon peeks down, trying not to laugh,
As vines start dancing, with no autograph.
"Is that a tango? Or a funky twist?"
The blooms all cheer, "We'll add it to our list!"

So sway and twirl beneath soft silver light,
Where flowers and vines make everything bright.
Their secret serenades echo through night,
In a world of delight, nothing feels right!

Echoes Beneath the Blossoms

Beneath the blossoms, a curious crew,
Chirps from crickets, and giggles anew.
A daisy declares, with petals so spry,
"Last week, a snail tried to fly in the sky!"

Beehives are buzzing with glee in their booth,
As daisies tease them, "Tell us the truth!"
One bee responds, with a wink on his wing,
"We never tell lies, just good honey bling!"

The flowers all ponder, and then they agree,
That laughter is sweeter than honey or tea.
Under each petal, a chuckle takes flight,
Creating a symphony, sparkly and bright!

Echoes of laughter, stretching like vines,
In the field full of joy, where everyone shines.
With memories captured in petals so fair,
Each giggle reminds us there's fun everywhere!

Twilight Murmurs in the Canopy

As twilight descends in the leafy domain,
The trees start to murmur, not fading or vain.
"Did you hear that? The sun took a fall!"
Chimes in a squirrel, with eyes big and tall.

The branches all rustle, sharing a thrill,
Of a rumor that blossoms are wearing a chill.
"Let's dress up the garden in sparkles and flair!"
Calls out a tulip; they're having a fair!

With laughter like petals, they spin and they sway,
In the canopy dance, where shadows can play.
"A party tonight, let's decorate bright!"
Sings a sweet breeze, giving all a delight.

So amidst the giggles, and magic they weave,
In the twilight's embrace, together they breathe.
The trees tell adventures, the flowers agree,
There's fun in the night, where they're all wild and free!

Shadows of Silken Petals

A squirrel skipped by, so spry and bold,
He thought he could steal our lunch from the fold.
But alas, he slipped on a slippery vine,
And fell with a plop — oh, how we did dine!

The petals above were drooping in glee,
As he scrambled back up, not so quick as a bee.
"I'll just grab a nut!" he huffed with a shout,
But we giggled in chorus — was that really a route?

In sunlight they shimmer, those flowers so fine,
But watch where you step — you might trip on a line!
The garden's a stage with laughter and cheer,
Where walls can't contain the delightful veneer.

A cat stretched and yawned, in a dainty ballet,
While mocking the antics of the squirrel's display.
The curtains of petals swayed to and fro,
As we chuckled and cheered for the show down below.

Conversations of the Climbing Vines

Up the trellis, the ivy takes flight,
With banter so cheeky, a real delight.
"You think you're the longest?" the clematis teased,
"But check out my reach, I'm perfectly pleased!"

The morning glories chimed in with a grin,
"But don't forget us when the day does begin!"
How they wrapped around, sharing tales of the night,
While sharing their secrets, both lofty and light.

Amidst all the giggles, the sunflowers stood tall,
"We're the stars of this show, you won't outshine us all!"
Yet vines only laughed, their climb far from done,
They twirled and they twisted, enjoying the fun.

As they argued and chatted in jubilant tones,
Creating a symphony of nature's own tones.
The garden became quite the raucous affair,
Where petals and leaves led a carnival fair.

Beneath the Purple Veil

A sly little mouse crept under the bloom,
Looking for snacks in this fragrant room.
With crumbs on his whiskers, he giggled aloud,
Thinking he was silent, quite the crafty crowd!

"Not so fast, there buddy!" chirruped a lark,
"You'll have to be sneaky, or you'll miss your mark!"
The flowers just chuckled, swaying with mirth,
As secrets and snacks filled this whimsical earth.

The breeze played a tune, oh what a delight,
As each tiny critter embraced the sweet night.
They gossiped and whispered, the petals would sway,
"What mischief will spring forth at the break of day?"

Underneath twinkling stars, they shared sweet tales,
Of daring adventures and quick little fails.
With laughter and joy, the garden would spin,
For joy underneath blossoms is where it begins.

Soliloquies of the Seasons

In springtime's embrace, with the sun's gentle wink,
The daisies debated, on what they should think.
"Should we bloom bright yellow or dress up in pink?"
They giggled and spun, oh, how could they blink?

Then summer arrived with a grand trumpet sound,
And the bumblebees buzzed, all spinning around.
"Who wears stripes better?" they bickered with flair,
As they danced with the daisies, without a care.

With autumn came colors — a vibrant display,
While leaves twirled and tumbled, they had much to say.
"Why so serious, friends? With laughter let's play!"
The trees shook their branches, laughing all day.

And winter, the joker, wrapped in a white shroud,
Sent snowflakes to tumble and twirl round the crowd.
Each season a player, they teased and they danced,
In the life of this garden — oh, wouldn't they prance!

Whirling Colors of Dusk

As twilight twirls in purple flair,
A squirrel skates on the old chair.
He thinks he's quite the daring chap,
But oh, he spills the acorn sap!

The sky's a canvas, wild and bright,
While clouds play peek-a-boo at night.
The trees chuckle, oh so sweet,
As fireflies start their little fleet.

The leaves giggle with a rustling cheer,
As crickets launch their symphonic beer.
In this madcap dance with nature's jest,
We laugh with colors that never rest.

So come, my friend, enjoy the show,
Where shadows play in sunset's glow.
With every twist, the laughter grows,
In this whimsical world, anything goes!

The Dance of Fragile Fragrance

A bloom with perfume, oh so grand,
Is caught in a jig, just like a band.
The bees all buzz, with a wiggle and a spin,
While petals twirl like they want to win!

The lilacs laugh, with a fragrant cheer,
But watch out for pollen, here comes a sneeze near!
Yet flies join in, doing the tango tease,
In this wacky garden, you beg them please.

The daisies roll in a grand pirouette,
While roses throw hats, like a wild duet.
And all the shrubs are nodding wise,
As laughter blooms under the sunny skies.

So let's stomp our feet in this fragrant spree,
With colors that burst and jokes for free.
Each flower knows how to spin and sway,
Join the party, let's dance the day away!

Voices Beneath the Overarching Canopy

Under the leaves, where shadows play,
The squirrels swap stories in a cheeky way.
A raccoon pipes in with a silly joke,
And all the owls hoot, "That's no hoax!"

The branches sway to their raucous song,
In a lively tune, where all belong.
"Who stole the acorns?" a crow caws loud,
As the tree trunk chuckles, so very proud.

A fox winks sly, with a knowing glance,
While ferns join in for the merriest dance.
The canopy shelters the laughter and glee,
As nature's fab five delight to be free.

So tilt your ear to the rustling air,
You'll find the world isn't quite so rare.
With each leafy laugh, the wild calls you near,
Join the chorus of whimsy, my dear!

Sighs of the Swaying Branches

The branches sway with a heavy sigh,
As squirrels munch nuts and let out a cry.
The wind teases leaves to dance and glide,
But caught in their play is a hummingbird's pride!

One branch claims, "I'm the best magician!"
While another retorts, "Please get in position!"
They twist and turn in a leafy ballet,
As the lizards enjoy from warm sun's ray.

The acorns bounce as they fall in bed,
A squirrel exclaims, "Look! My lunch is spread!"
Amidst such chaos, the laughter sings,
In the groovy world of nature's rings.

So here we are, where the tall trees sway,
With jokes and giggles brightening the day.
Each sigh's a chuckle, each rustle a tease,
In this playful forest, we dance with ease!

Hushed Tales from the Garden

In the dark of night, frogs hold court,
Debating who's the best at sport.
One claims to leap with the best of flair,
While crickets giggle, just sitting there.

The daisies gossip, all in a row,
About the beetle who danced in tow.
He slipped and tumbled, a comic sight,
Rolling away just before the light.

A snail took a ride on a ladybug's back,
Zooming along like a wild hack.
"Faster!" he yelled, as they whirled 'round,
But trails of slime were quickly found.

The moon collects secrets, oh so sly,
As mice pull pranks under the sky.
Each twig a stage, each leaf a screen,
In this playful realm, madness is seen.

Beneath the Cascading Blooms

Under blooms that hang low and wide,
The bees throw jokes like a wild ride.
"Hey, flower! You think you're so sweet?"
Buzzing with laughter, they skip to the beat.

A butterfly frets about her bad hair,
While ants create fashion, beyond compare.
With leaves as their garments, they strut and preen,
On this floral runway, the best you've seen.

A squirrel, with nuts, pulls a prank so grand,
Feigning drop-offs—it's all unplanned.
The others just chuckle, rolled on the ground,
While acorn confetti falls all around.

Each petal's a punchline; each stem has a tale,
In a garden where joy, never can fail.
Life's light-hearted moments play on repeat,
When nature's ensemble takes to the street.

The Breath of Enchanted Vines

Grapes giggle softly, swinging in cheer,
Planning a party, but who will be here?
"Let's invite the bees and that old wise owl,
And the raccoon who sneaks growls like a pro!"

Vines twist and tangle, forming a dance,
While worms try to keep up, taking a chance.
"Left foot, then right! No, wait—start again!"
And crickets applaud, with their tiny zen.

A hedgehog rolls in, all puffed up and sly,
"Who knew I could boogie? Just give it a try!"
As laughter erupts like bubbles in a drink,
Nature's sweet humor brings smiles with a wink.

Even the rocks join, with a thud and a roll,
Stones shaking hard, just to feel the whole.
In this world of laughter, joy never resigns,
Creating delight with each twist of the vines.

Silken Echoes of the Evening

When dusk creeps in, spirits take wing,
As fireflies gather to dance and sing.
"Who's got the glowiest glow?" they declare,
And a bumblebee chuckles, "Not me, I swear!"

The shadows stretch out, crafting silly views,
As roses tell tales with their vibrant hues.
"Look at that daffodil, dressed in his best!"
As laughter erupts with a floral fest.

Even the stars twinkle in delight,
What's a show without a quirky knight?
A grasshopper hops on the moon's silver beam,
Saying he's auditioning for the dream team.

The petals converse, with giggles and glee,
Underneath the sky, wild and free.
So raise your voice, let the laughter ring,
For nature holds secrets, enchanting and zing!

Hushed Lullabies in the Garden

In the garden, the gnomes stand tall,
With hats too big and pants too small.
They gossip softly, trade silly tales,
Of mischievous squirrels and their funny fails.

Butterflies flutter, a comical sight,
In a race with the bees, they take flight.
The daisies giggle, they share a glance,
As the daisies whisper, "Let's start a dance!"

The carrots wear glasses, quite dapper indeed,
Trying to read while they nibble on seed.
The tomatoes chuckle, round and plump,
"Let's form a band—let's make some thump!"

So in this patch, where laughter grows,
The flowers are jesters, and joy overflows.
With every bloom, a punchline appears,
In this garden, we toast to our cheers!

Memory's Veil in Purple Haze

Under purple skies, the memories sway,
Like forgetful bees, they've lost their way.
With a giggle, the lilacs spill their tea,
"Oh, what did he say? Was it '3' or '3G'?"

The daisies debate on the best kind of hat,
While roses roll eyes at the jester, a cat.
"Let's have a feast!" the petunias exclaim,
"Bring us some snacks, and we'll play a game!"

Giggling sunflowers sway in the breeze,
They outrun the shade, with such elegant ease.
"Let's chase the raindrops, oh what a spree!"
They splash and they dash, all wild and free.

At sundown, they chuckle, their day nearly done,
In memory's haze, they've had such fun.
With laughter so sweet, under stars' gaze,
These buds of joy live in memory's maze.

Beneath the Floral Archway

Beneath the blooms where the mischief stirs,
The vines tell secrets in gentle purrs.
A caterpillar laughs, can't keep still,
Dreaming of wings, sharing such thrill.

Around the corner, the foxgloves sing,
With petals like bells, what joy they bring!
They chat about gossip, flower to flower,
"Did you see that bee? He's lost his power!"

A shady spot where the squirrels convene,
Playing with acorns, acting so serene.
"Life's a jest, let's play hide and seek!"
With a wag of their tails, they sneak and peek.

"Oh, look at the tulips, they think they're the best!"
They boast and they bicker, never a rest.
Yet under this arch, amidst laughter wide,
Every flower knows it's a fun-filled ride!

Tangles of Time and Nature

In a tangle of vines, the time's gone awry,
The clock's melting down, oh my oh my!
The daisies dressed up, all fancy and bright,
In a fashion show, what a silly sight!

"Why wear a crown when you can wear leaves?"
A bold sunflower shouts, "Who needs the thieves?"
The clovers all giggle, their luck is so grand,
'Paw-sitively charming' is their little band!

The ivy is laughing, she climbs up with flair,
"Time lost its grip, it's floatin' in air!"
"Just pluck a few dreams, and stir them with glee,
Adventure awaits, come dance with me!"

So let's twirl through the garden with glee and with gabs,
With our floral friends, we'll steal all the jabs.
In this tangled wonder, where fun is the goal,
Nature's a jester, with a free-spirited soul!

Conversations with the Moonlit Petals

Under a sky of shimmering light,
The flowers gossip through the night.
One says, 'Did you hear the bee?
He stole my pollen, how rude can he be?'

Petals giggle as moonbeams play,
They swap their stories, come what may.
A daisy blushes, 'I think it's fair,
I once danced with a breeze in the air!'

The violets chirp, full of delight,
'We chased the stars till morning light!'
They tease the roses, quite in a jam,
'You're all thorns and no sense of glam!'

Laughter echoes in the night's embrace,
As garden blooms share their funny grace.
With every bud, a tale unspools,
In the moon's glow, they swap all the jewels.

When Blossoms Speak in Silence

In a garden where secrets grow,
The blooms hold meetings, quite the show.
'The tulips asked why I can't stand tall,
It's because I'm stuffed with too much pollen, that's all!'

The lilies giggle, 'Oh, don't you know?
We love to dance when the breezes blow!'
But the daisies shout, 'That's not quite true,
Every time we twirl, we get covered in dew!'

At midnight hour, petals softly laugh,
'Why did the rose fall? Too much bath!'
They plot and plan, with petals bright,
As crickets play their tunes in the night.

With quiet charm, they share their cheer,
Each petal loves to lend a ear.
In their silent whispers, a funny song,
A symphony of blooms, where all belong.

Ghosts of the Garden's Heart

Among the greens, there's a tale to tell,
Of flowers that bloom and giggle quite well.
'Look at those daisies, acting so spry,
Just because they think they are the reason for the sky!'

The snapdragons snicker, 'We'd frighten a ghost!
Though we're more like jesters, we laugh the most!'
Petals rattle, as if the breeze can hear,
Their humor wafts, quite light and clear.

Some say the thorns are quite the jest,
Always poking fun, never let them rest!
But as the shadows creep and blend,
Even the floral spirits can pretend.

They share their stories, bold and bright,
With giggles that linger deep in the night.
For in this garden, with its playful art,
The blooms dance along, the ghosts of the heart.

Petals that Paint the Silence

In a patch of color, whispers arise,
Petals discuss their crafty disguise.
'I wear a shade that steals the light,
While you wear spots, so bold and bright!'

The marigolds chuckle, 'Oh what a game,
Trying to outshine the sun, oh so tame!'
They sway and giggle under clear skies,
'Sunshine must be blind, oh what a surprise!'

With tickles of wind, the blooms take a spin,
Falling over petal-pranks, they all join in.
The garden burst forth with laughter and cheer,
As colors of fun fill the atmosphere.

So here's to petals, clever and sly,
In silence they paint a joke on the sky.
With every giggle, every chat,
They brighten the world, just look at that!

www.ingramcontent.com/pod-product-compliance
Lightning Source LLC
Chambersburg PA
CBHW072138200426
43209CB00050B/113